Fragile

and

The World Around Me

by

D. Green

PublishNation
www.publishnation.co.uk

Introduction

As I was growing up I lost myself along the way, and never knew who I was meant to be. I struggled with dyslexia from an early age and this caused me to feel isolated, as I had problems communicating with my peers. My experience of learning to adapt and develop the skills to gain my academic qualifications led me to help others. This ability gave me a professional career of fourteen years in the care industry.

Now, at the ripe old age of thirty-three, after needing to stop work due to ill health, I have accidentally stumbled across a way of expressing my emotions through words. When I was young I never knew I possessed this talent, or that I had the power to help others through their life journey with words. This concern inspired me to write about my journey with a chronic disease that few understand or see. It also describes the many journeys I have travelled through in life that everyone can relate to.

I want people to understand and learn what it feels like to walk in someone else's shoes. We all struggle daily with our own issues, although many do not look at the big picture. Living with a chronic disease, being the carer of someone with a disease, or being a family member of someone with a disease makes life all the more demanding. We sometimes need a gentle reminder that often these issues are outside a person's control and are not of their own making.

This thinking led me to watch the world and the people I see daily. Through love, loss, pain, and many lessons life throws at people throughout the world this gave me the insight to write about what I observed from a perspective of concern

1

and respect for many who suffer in silence. All the words I wrote naturally formed themselves into poems.

I hope that *Fragile body and the world around me* will give everyone who lives their life in silence a voice, the courage, and the inspiration to battle on, or to stand up and tell the world about their hardest times. With my poems I hope to show the human race that there are no two different people. We all experience the same hardships in life. Because you and I are really the same.

About the Author

I have suffered with multiple sclerosis, which has dealt me some massive blows, for fourteen years. A year ago I started writing after retiring from work at the very ripe old age of thirty-three, just to express how I felt in myself and the constant marathons I have run through life. And no, this has not all been plain sailing, but I have learned many valuable lessons that come with the gains and losses due to living with a chronic disease.

About this Book

Fragile body and the world around me delves into my subconscious but then conscious mind. It is about the long-fought battles with chronic diseases that many never come to see or understand. It has brought me some great success in love and also some great loss.

Then it opened my eyes to the rest of the world's struggles, the pain and loss that many suffer from in silence without a voice, and the hardships that many live with daily. You will all be able to relate to this book, as it is *our* voice.

On the Edge of Life

Falling from the sky faster than light
I woke in a room of sea-blue uniforms

What has become of the young man in his prime?

Standing by his side, gazing right through him
Wondering what events brought him there
I scanned the room where I had become invisible
To the traffic of sea-blue uniforms

With my ears deaf to all the noise that once was
A tube hung from my mouth, which had once made such
spirited remarks
Detached my eyes had become from the scene before me
My invisible self, pondering who this could be

A sharp pain rose from inside
It hit me with such pace and venom

This was me, the young man in his prime

I looked so pale and drained as I lay there
So helpless inside

A coma of peace stood by my side
I thought now that my time had come
To meet my maker

With such haste I gasped for breath and then woke

From the nightmare inside

Lost Love

I woke up again today with you in my thoughts
It was a struggle to fix my sights on anything else
So I came to one place in this world

I feel at peace where the land meets the sea
And the constant breeze warms my soul

With time maybe I will be able to heal myself
Therefore I will always have amazing memories with you
forever

I regret not loving you harder every day by my side
You will always hold that special place in my heart of hearts

Remembrance

A bugle plays once more
The last post we hear
Streams of poppies fill their arms
We remember all the fallen
From past but also present days

All the valiant men who gave their lives
For the freedom of our country
With a wreath in hand veterans play
One final salute
For the fallen comrades in arms
As brothers they once stood
But now
They have only respect to pay
For the sacrifice given

Flags lowered to half mast as a sign that
We will not forget
The world stands still for a minute

So we all remember who they were
With pride in our hearts
We have become eternally grateful
For everything you gave
So long may your legacies live on
In the nation you inspired

Numb Hands

The Simple Things You Miss That You Once Took for Granted

So no longer are you able to run
The hands of yours through your partner's hair

So now you've lost another simple pleasure
Of feeling her soft hair glide through your fingers

Even though they remain curled into a ball
With the deformities this body shows
As it carries abnormal lesions
That have come to control everything

You have tried to touch and hold
But no longer do they listen

Meanwhile, rebels dance to their own tunes

"I carry my scars with pride for all to see
As they are constant reminders of the battles I've won"

Once Again

It's come again so soon
Why has this become me again?

No sooner have I healed than it has reared that ugly head
again
Has legs that have become an alien form

A twitch I felt struck down in my face
The suffering inside felt dull
However, it beats with an immense pace

With such haste
I have become stuck again in the whirlwind of this vile disease
It has swallowed me whole
Who have I become?

But now the struggle has gone inside once more
With no slowing down in sight
It keeps raging on
Inflicting so much destruction of the former man in me

A shadow again descends on the control I once saw
Will an easier time show itself at last?

First the insects must leave my destroyed body
Then I might find the strength once more to face this world

So until then I will find comfort in the shadows
My last hope has left my future for now

Never Before

Never before has a love appeared like an engulfing flame
Ripping through one spirit

Never before has he wanted anyone so much
That she spends an eternity running through his heart

Never before has he seen a future with the one
He would die for any time in his life

Never before has he shown all his flaws
However, he will forever owe more to her

Never before has he been attracted to such a beauty
As the beauty who stands right before his eyes

Never before has he felt this much love
He will show her every day what he means

Never before has he found someone
Who completes him in every way like she does

Never before has he wanted love so pure
Until the day she walked through the door

Hero

A hero once stood, but the world has forgotten him now
So a solemn man stands alone
While rain pours on his distorted soul

Where has he come from? And where does he go?

No one knows, but only who he has become
The expression that he wears on his face
Tells a million stories
And the pain that shows in his sombre eyes
Tells of the loss he has suffered inside

The ghastly world keeps on spinning
But he will stay still inside
Every memory flashes
So lucidly before his eyes
For none he wants to see
As life drains from his exhausted body
Standing in a minefield once more

There he remains standing
As still as ice
Remembering them all
From the days that have passed
There will be one final salute
For his fallen brother in arms as the world spins on by

Weary Legs

My legs crumbling underneath me
Becoming more unbalanced with every step I take
Placing one foot in front of the other
As my attached limbs feel so numb
On every surface they strike upon

So my stride moves to more of a shuffle
Visually displaying my wobbly glitch
Like a foal trying to walk for the very first time

But the gawky looks of awkwardness
Make me grow embarrassed
Causing me to walk faster
Becoming clumsier
Making my feet collide together

As I then plummet to the floor
In a heap of mess

"The desperation of humanity lay in this unforgiving world"

My Enemy

I close my eyes for a minute, nearly feeling normal
My mind is shattered and broken inside
This thing I have controls my every thought
Like a deluded illness running free inside

I try to brush it aside, then live again
For it stops me in my tracks
As it will not beat me it only makes my mind go crazy inside
No rational thoughts to clear my doubt of suspicious intent
This thing I have rampages on inside

My worst enemy I have become
Who I hold at the core of me
Until this day my demons will carry on their fury
A war zone my mind has become
Colours so vivid still in pictures of the destruction in me
Slowly my mind repairs, but the scars of damage will stay
within me
So for now I must live to fight another day

Noticed

Don't stutter
She noticed you

Stand as still as a statue
She might pass by

She perceives all the colours of affection with her eyes

Such beauty she carries
So vibrantly on her shoulders

Never have you seen someone so bold

Her graceful stance of attractiveness invites you in

The hands she holds
Glide through any storm that confronts her

A need of impulse rises
From inside your vessel

But you can only gaze
Upon her unknown spirit

The craving you have to chase her turns you into
A frenzy of passion
The one you must have become

Hope

Newly found hope crushed out of every bone in her
uninhabited body
The deluded plague rages in her own mind
She never thought this would become her life
Closer she looks, but the world remains behind these four
walls

Suddenly she thinks, *I may never hold my dearest loves again*
So tears roll from her empty spheres of ice

A wife, once a mother, isolated from a home she holds so dear
No hope seen at any new sunrise in this desolate place
A freedom denied despite the innocence of this caged mother

Prayers stay unanswered from a powerful nation
A woman denied every vain hope of happiness in this world

"My spirit will fly high on the winds
Carrying me to brighter places"

Relapse

As I lie in bed
My legs don't feel mine
A marathon I've just run
But no finish line in sight
A lightning bolt I feel
That time has come again
Its ghastly head has reared up once more

As I battle with the discomfort
I fix my sights on my strength inside
Struggling to my weary legs again
As I gaze in the mirror
A shadow of the former man I once was I saw

What's destined for me I do not know
But the war inside continues on
Knowing this I will fight on
This nasty illness will not ruin what I have inside

So I now know I might merely exist
But with this vile disease I can still truly exist

The legs that were not mine dance once more
The day has come when I must face my foes
As this has become my only friend

Everything I dreamed of

She touched my heart
I have become what she desires inside

I touched her soul so she has become what I dreamed of

My soulmate I have found
And I am her soulmate too
A true friend I once dreamed of I have found
So perfect in every way but with scars inside

She sits but stares
So intense her love

My soul flickers then dances with her in sight
The one true north I have become for her
A love so pure I have found and become
The rage of passion in each of our hearts
For two hearts have left their dwelling places
And have become one

The rock of my life she has become
So that the the pain inside will dwindle away

A future so bright now shines on us
The resting place for my heart she holds with hers

My one true love I want forever
Until my dying breath I will hold it forever

Massacre

Massacre my nerves
Blocking every connection
To my breathing bag of bones
As I lie paralysed inside
With only a feeling of exhaustion
Keeping me collapsed on this spot

Maybe if I found some energy
I would have the power to move
But this vicious disorder has hacked away at
All my strength
For what feels like a lifetime
It leaves and breaks
From every sensation that once occupied
This vibrant spirit

Missing Mother

Tormented by her captors
Seen by millions
But she only becomes her own tormentor
When she loses her small child

About time people sat up and
Listened to the story of a missing mother

Only she feels the pain that rips inside her heart
The mental anguish she feels
With every passing thought
A grief she carries for her one wish

To embrace the one thing she wants to hold so near
The love seen in pictures so pure
Then seen by the millions

She still sits isolated in a cage in a land not her home

Why has she been left so long to become her own tormentor?
For a society fighting for the freedom of a missing mother

*"My spirit will fly high on the winds
Carrying me to brighter places"*

Vile Disease

I stumble
I can feel the eyes of a thousand strangers
Pierce through me

She steadies me
But my legs don't work any more
Slowly she walks beside me
Her grip getting tighter

I stumble again
This vile disease has a grip of me
I fight against it with all my might
But my body fights no more

This horrid disease controls me now
But only for a while

My head held high
I reach for my aids
But my hands don't want to work any more

Still the eyes of a thousand strangers
Pierce through me
A cripple
I feel fated by this vile disease

I once stood a man with pride inside
Now I have become broken within

This vile disease controls me now
But only for a while

Soon the light will come
Then
I will bid my oldest friend farewell

Love

Follow me to the brink of life with your tenderness
I will show you everything in my life
Be careful, though, my love

It might become so bright
Because this you taught me of love
Vivid colours now merge into one
Telling our story

Fond memories of years together I hold in me
Never let this emotion die inside us
For I have many more years of love
To give you

Commanded

As the hourglass slowly moves on Watch it
It takes me over again
So my free movements turn to stone
Which infuriates my mind's command

For my every sense is no longer mine
But is commanded by
This deep-rooted defect I am infested with
That has been placed in me
Which leaves me feeling bizarre

As my feet bounce in the air as if I am walking on the moon
For now I just want ordinary back

Then again
Feeling peculiar is marvellous

Bringing me total uniqueness
Making me a rare individual

As I feel like I'm in outer space
But on earth

Grief

Stay with me
I am so cold
Just a little longer
My beloved
A few seconds
Are all we have left

Close your eyes, Precious
Remembering all our glory days

Slowly succumb to
Whatever it has in store
Embrace it
For this will be your next chapter

For all our time together
I have always cherished you
But for the rest of the time
I will still love you

My heart is breaking with sorrow
For I will never hold you again

"Blood flows down the river
For love in our hearts
Sometimes bleeds out"

Depression

A young statue of a man raised above the world to see
Pinned to one spot by the stone from within

Lost between two worlds he had become
No time for wondering or even for contemplating

How did he ever struggle to hear?
No sight left for seeing the wonders of our world

So a touch can come no more from his stone hands
A slumbering in the state of his mind will show once more

But once more a yearning he feels to be semi-normal
A sudden move

The once solid stone
Shows a crack at last

Colour returns with such clarity
Defining everything in sight

A depression that once was lifts finally
Which shows many a crack
Of the scars in this distorted soul

Breathe

Let's breathe together with our lives
Inhale all of me in
Filling your lungs
In return I will breathe all of you in
So we can soar together
Like never before

Fill my body with so much joy
Then gently touch my face
So I will always remember your touch

But then I will navigate your body
Touching every inch of you

Delicately place your lips on mine
So I know how soft they feel

Then let me run my fingers through your hair
So I know how it falls

But let me be the one who pulls you closer
On to your toes

Take Me

Come on, take me now
Do what you want

For I have no fight left
Within my aching body

So now it might never be mine any more
But please leave my brain intact

Then I will still be able to dream
Of running and playing in the wilderness
That much my imagination still brings me
With every new moon that shines
On a life that is now so empty

As this bed has become
My only dream comfort

Mother's Freedom

She has lost her life with freedom
Inside in a world she trusted
Now her only friend
These steel rods of iron have become
But still time rolls on
For this caged mother

So will she stay in a hostile land
With torture in sight
No day passes without pain in her heart
For the loved ones she holds so close

As days roll into one
There remains no end in sight
She becomes fearful
At every thought of freedom

The hope of being close to loved ones
Slowly dies inside
There is a sadness that lies so deep
For a daughter she once adored

She will only see light through the bars
Which keep her from a life she once lived
So this struggle of her life
Will carry on until the world takes note

"Tonight, you are everything
Tomorrow you might become nothing"

Demons Within

Creeping on the haze of a shadow
No one ever wants monsters
Lurking in the dark

But monsters are demons of every person in sight
Just lingering
Waiting for the chaos to start

Many have seen their demons within
But few ever let them roam
So freely outside

The ones that play are peaceful in spirit
So friends they must become
To survive inside

The monsters now seem not so tragic
Running happily around me
As I grasp their hands

Soon will come the time for them
To spread their wings
Then fly

Entice

Never has he seen such vibrant beauty before
So will he stare right into her slowly dying heart
Possessed by the wish of love

He tries in every way to entice her longing gaze
So damaged she has become that no man sees
But his eyes full of love for her
See the scars within

He felt the cold in her voice descend over his soul
But never would he give up the chase for her
As he saw a loving soul held behind barriers of steel

She must be conquered
Then shown love once more

Then one day he saw glowing warmth
Creeping out from within her
Finally a new-found wish that she wanted to be had risen
And smiles like the brightest stars
Beamed across her once sombre face

Waves

The waves are coming
Crashing into my weakness
Which has only come along
Because of this plague you're
Riddled with
That you've carried inside
Throughout the many years
I have walked this world

But no more do I want
To be broken down
By these corrosives waves That taunt the feelings
Of every awareness
You've come to miss

You wait for the waves
To go back to the sea
So our bodies may start to repair them

My Child

Every day my child hurts
For I have been stupid
But only once

I remember the last time
We laid eyes on each other
Like it was only yesterday
Which was too many years ago

I should never have let you go from my side
And so I will be reminded daily
By the sorrow in my life

Through pictures I see of you growing
I gather some warmth
Knowing you are loved

But the pain will always stay, dear child
For one day I hope we will meet again

"Take me back
Now take me back
To when life was no worry"

Crushed Shell

Once a storm, it now grows into a full-blown hurricane
The cold creeps up inwards, running in my veins
Crippling every move deep inside

The strength I need slowly dying in my weary, depleted limbs
Some courage left slowly bleeds out of every possible orifice
With no sign that I may be strong enough to swim
These choppy waters once more
So I need the strength of a dear loved one to pull me through
once again

The man standing before me with pain in his sombre eyes
Just becomes me again

With a dull ache inside this crushed shell of this man
Who has come to exist only for now

Should I say it has beaten me?

But my brain fights with every movement inside
My mind is courageous, and will only make me fight for
another day

Captured

A girl sat across from me who saw everything I was

Deep yet mysteriously dancing eyes you held from there
Your smile spoke a hundred feelings to me
But your eyes spoke a million times more

Your laugh was infectious beyond any yearning I held for you
I remember longing to wrap myself in your loving web
Taking one deep breath in a while you breathed life through
me

So gentle your voice sang every time you came near
A warm glow shone over your entire surroundings
Outlining your soul to me

Then the way you ran your hands through your hair
So affectionately towards me

Shall I say that this was the day you captured then stole my
heart?

Numbness

This numbness creeps up
On my body once more
To linger on my surface

Letting me know that it is ready to inflict
Such carnage on my actions
With the most disastrous agony
It always brings with it

As no pain goes unnoticed
In my frail interior
Which I've contended with
For such a lengthy time
That I have battled with in my liveliness

So once more I will shed blood inside
Fighting this enemy and
Rising from my smouldering ashes

Caged Mother

She sits in her cage
Unconditional love flows through her dying heart

For a small child who she remembers so fondly
Plays on every heartstring

A child is lost
Running free in her soul
Creating every tear inside

The strength she needs to find
Pulls on her every tormented thought

She must survive another day in this nightmare place

Longing for one last embrace from her crushed life
She prays
A broken mind sits by her side

No one listens
So depression rages on

Thoughts of living through this nightmare
Destroy her day by day
As the missing piece of her jigsaw
Lies inside her
The small child who has become her

"A little of you
Trapped inside of me"

Uncontrolled Destiny

The uncontrolled destiny of my life
Thrown into a terminal decline with a chronic disease

Lingering in the depths
Waiting to strike with such force
And then with venom, its friend

Such devastation is caused by crippling every signal inside
All short circuits shown
Although there is no repair in sight

Many have seen before being reduced to
Just merely existing vessels

For the battle no one sees
Of the chronic disease within
That only the host knows

The long-fought war will remain

Desire

Love grows in a barren place
That none have ever before touched
A bleak heart, slowly brought back from the brink of darkness
That has been hidden for too long

Shall I say it is a love nurtured by you
With love that blossomed because of you?

An overwhelming desire appears
At every look from inside you

Nevertheless, every minute of every day
The need for you drives me to madness

My love for you grows every day
So I will love you more

As I savour every memory of you
My mind becomes active again

The thought of loving you more
Excites my ever-aching heartstrings
You have become me for now
Until forever

I shall hold your love so near to me
That I will never let go of you

MS

Your electrical pulsating currents
Play an instrumental tune inside
That makes me twitch to your sound

But none see my moves from outside
For the odd occasional jerk
Makes me look like a faulty robot
That's malfunctioning due to being wired wrong
Which all come to look at with the most
Unwanted stares that no one likes

So I try to break your moves inside me
But you keep thrashing about
Moving unpleasantly like never before

And so now I try to move in tune with you
To make it look natural to every passer-by
But my body starts jigging more
As you pick up the beat of your tune

Five Hundred Days

Five hundred days it has been
Since she last held her rock
The so-called life once led by her
Has now become a dream

A child she once held so tightly with love
She has become a stranger to
All the colours of happier days
Fade into one livid grey haze
No sun in sight to bring delivery
From this constantly dreaded place

A world outside stands beside you
For one we have become

Close your eyes for a minute
So you can sees how dark
It has become
In the shattered mother's mind

All our strength we pass to you
With hope of justice in sight
But all our love we give you
For the strength you need to fight

"Time can slowly mend you
But real love can make you fly again"

Kiss Goodbye

Now hear the silent 2.3 million voices cry
About their invisible illness
Continually discriminated against
Judgment thrown from every angle in sight

The world needs to know
Of this heavy burden
They carry so proudly

So we will kiss goodbye to it from every nation
Then hopefully be granted a cure
To rid the world of this

But until that time we unite as one family With squads of
supporters planted
All over the world

For all to see what amazing people these are

Fragile Heart

Rip it out of me, dear
Tear it out from me

Now stamp all over it
Nothing has come to matter

Crush it under your heel
I don't need it any more

See, I told you it was fragile
Make it bleed
Make it ooze red
See, I am nothing to you

Now pick it up and give it back
For that is the piece I gave to you

Now leave and walk away from me
Then never turn back to look at me
For I am broken by you

See, I don't need a heart in this cold world

Be Her

Be her hope
Be her strength
Be her voice, as she cannot be heard
Be the love in her daughter's heart
Be the compass she needs by her side

Be as one for her freedom now
Be the reason we will never forget
Be the fighting world they never expected

Be the wind to carry her home
Be the sun to brighten her day
Be her reason for never giving up
Be the story for all the world to hear
Be together for the missing mother

Pain

Turn that screw a bit harder
I cannot feel it

You have hurt me more than this
Is that all the pain you have for me?

Come on
Inflict some more
I am ready to move to the next stage

I have battled for too many years with you
Having lost more than won

So now I am ready to be defeated again
But will rise stronger than before

Every time you knock me down
I will stand to face you again

So I never underestimate my courage
For I will win again one day

"Love will find you under any dark cloud
Returning the light to your life so we can see it once more"

Orange Warrior

Hear my battle cry from the warrior inside
Listen to my beating heart of war drums
Watch as I slay everything evil inside and slash it out of me

The courage I possess will see me rise whenever I fall
My pride only I will carry on my shoulders
Such strength I will show at anything thrown in my way

For I am an orange warrior

My Prayer

Like a prayer he holds so near she's become
One he will not be parted from
The conviction of his heart is here
While she holds everything of him with her heart so near

Never has his damaged core seen love
Never before has his destiny been so clear

An infectious desire she has become
The final chapter of his life he longs to spend with her
A force so strong she holds so close with him
For this swelling heart she wears with pride

He will continue to fix with stars in sight
A love with honour has engulfed him
Her passion has been imprinted on his heart by her

The darkness that once was now light fills beside him
The gentleness of his soul only matured with her

A guide she has formed for him
With love he only sees in her

Spasms

Health gradually being dragged down
To the depths of no return

For the spasms constantly bounce around
And leave many disabled muscles

But these spasms never seem to pass on by
As more show every day with no break

They cause so many uncomfortable looks
Then judged I am because I am different

But in myself I know I am special
Because no one else can walk in these shoes

That's why I was given this
To prove to the world

That you can still be normal and thrive
Through anything you have been given to deal with

Don't Forget

Kneel down
Touch the ground
I can feel you there
Only not in my arms

Wait for me now
I will be following you soon
Don't forget me
So we can find each other again

The only time I see you
Is in my dreams
Come back to me
Then hold me tight once more

For this life has drained away
And filled with emptiness
Since you departed

"We were born with two different souls
That ignited into the wildest fires nearby"

The Game

So the game has started once more
A paranoid presence I shall feel from here
Every feeling has slowly died through the destruction of me

Finally darkness covers my body
No figures I see through the light that shows
The fragile state of my mind returns once more

A game I don't want to play any more rages on
The cry for help comes from deep within

A hurtful pain that needs to fade so fast
Why has this become me again?

I don't want this to be me any more
Slowly I am dying inside my tormented mind
A cold metal presses against my skin

Do I hesitate to inflict more pain
Or should I watch my veins become death?
I need to find some strength

Cerebral Hemisphere

I will slowly lose my voice
As these insects are colonising
My left cerebral hemisphere
With many new nests coming to light

But then I should be more worried
About my body's motor functions
Which will become only a memory
Of happier times
When I could do
Whatever I happened to want

So for now I will build my defences
Ready for the onslaught of attack after attack
Which I will battle to keep at bay
As I have always been the most fearsome fighter
With the strength of ten thousand warriors

So show me your best warrior, old friend
Then watch me rise to victory again

Dream

So close to me I feel her warmth
She holds me near so I can see all
I notice burning love inside her soul

Until this day a dream she was
Now that dream breathes with me

Eyes alight
Which I have never seen before

So in return a piece of me she will see and hold
With a time so precious
That we will share in the hearts of ours

We have become, every waking hour
For one another

Newborn

I remember your eyes when they first opened
The smallest of fingers clenched around my life

The uncontrollable love that was raised from my roots
By the way you nestled into my arms for the love you craved

Followed every milestone with sheer delight
Then danced with you in my arms while holding you so tight

A love you showed me in return through your tiny heart
Pictures I see of your smile bring me such joy

Then a promise I will make to never give up
For my child you will be forever

"Trust those who hold your heart with love
For these are the real bearers of your happiness"

Psychosis

Her eyes start to flicker again
It's time for the voices that have penetrated into her deep soul
To play so many roles that no one ever wants
As a twitch strikes through her surroundings
Her eyes must roll once more

Many a person is seen in the vessel she has become
At this time no one can help
Or even come close to what she is going through here

A violent tongue strikes out while her eyes
Fill with such unforgiving rage
The volatile storm she is passing through
Picks up speed with so much haste

An unconscious mind now shines
For she has become so peaceful with eyes closed

Only then will her eyes return to the former way she looked at
you
So true

Never Love Again

I will never love again
As you were the last love I ever wanted
I will now be alone forever
Out of respect for our love

I will never be able to get rid of this myself

Like the sun will never leave the moon
I will never make you leave my heart
This has always been your place

So let your memories fill me with joy
Until the end of time
Then I will be at peace
Knowing you were my last love

Darkness

It was a weary time
Darkness fell around him

A cold wind brushes his face

It was a familiar place
But he looked so lost

By his side stands the figure
Of a lifeless person
Once possessed by many a devil

So still the air has become
The colours of day
Had faded into darkness
Which clung close
To his empty heart

No one noticed him
Leave the world behind
So torn
By the fragile life he had led

Critical of any judgement
Pressed against his mind
With lasting disappointment
From failing at every step in life
Beside the belief
That no good would come to pass

So paranoia sits hand in hand
With every fleeting thought
That presents
With no meaningful insight

Then joy fills his heart
As devils fly by
The time comes to live
With the magical world again

"Teach me how to love again
Because I have become so damaged inside"

Mind Functions

I am sometimes lost
My mind functions are broken
You expect words
But just get silence
As the only response

I hear what you say
But never fully understand
That's when I feel stupid
No questions I ask
My mind knows stuff
But not common conversations

I try so hard to speak openly
But no words I find
Then I become so vacant
With 'Sorry' the only remark I have
Constant frustration
At my own mind's processes

I cannot cope

Then my mind goes
On random detours
About any situation
That confronts me in life
My wandering eyes show
I am searching for an answer
But none I find

Then beside you I am stupid
So my communication lacks conviction

I ask many times then look at you
Then I get back nothing but emptiness

Whole Again

I need to be whole again
Which no longer do I feel
Each day I write
Thinking ink touching my pages will help

For my body needs something
Unsure of what any more

I felt myself lose my only compass I ever found
To guide me in this dreadful world
However, I always come back to my windy spot
Where it has brought me so much peace in the past

This time just eternal memories I see everywhere I look
I once had the most treasured thing
This world could give the love of another
But no more do I have love

Then I turn
Not knowing where to go
For I never got to share

One last tender kiss
Or a warm embrace

Death

The thought of death becoming your only friend
As cold metal presses against your skin
Red starts to run from your cold body walls

Now comes the time
There is no turning back

You have travelled too far this time
With no saviour
While the world's light before you
Gets dimmer and dimmer again

What a waste of a young, talented life
They will write

So close your eyes for one last time
Though you will never know when you will depart

"Never underestimate dreams
Dreams can define who we can be"

Own Worst Enemy

He has become his own worst enemy
A once honest man lost in his own web
Spiralling out of control again for all to see
This is not who he is
Or who he wants to be

An honest man he wishes would come back
Now more than ever
The one who spoke with a truthful tongue
Who never had a doubt in his mind
Without true conviction

Where have you gone, old friend?
Come forth so you can take control

Until I find you again
This daily struggle to live will carry on

Just Remember

Just remember I saw you

For the first time in your life
Someone saw you

I looked right into your beauty
Stared straight at your flaws
Then stood by your side
Through every hurdle you faced

I was there holding your hand
My grip is getting tighter
To make sure you never fall

Yet this chapter has closed
Without being finished

For now you have fallen
Because I'm not there any more

Which has killed me every day since

Devils

Watch for the devils in life
They dress like you and me

Their faces may seem pleasant
Though their tempers will turn nasty
The tongues they have hiss poison

Be sure, though
To watch for those eyes
They will draw you in
Then take your soul
Then you will become
Under their control

With no returning
To what you were before
So now I tell you
Step carefully
Through this world

"Universes can collide by bringing two souls together
Never doubting that we are not destined to be together"

Expressions

My expressions may look blank
But that's because you never see
What I have to fight against every day

So bleak have become my emotions
But so hardened my strength to rise another day
For I have become my own saviour in the messed-up world I
see

Now stand again with pride held high
Then start to walk your road alone

Sometimes no one ever comes to understand what
You fight with every day inside

I See You

I see you but so quickly you go
I search behind every closed door
I run back to the mirror
I see you again
That flickering smile

Then you disappear from me

I turn on every light to see you better
But no more do I see you
I feel your warm, gentle breath on my neck

Then you disappear once more
Where are you now showing yourself?

Then I hear the sound of you giggling
But that's coming from deep within
For what is happening in me?
Only you will know the memories left
Running in me

Then you disappear once more

Borrowed Time

We live on borrowed time every day
Not knowing when our story will end

So much love for today
But keep respect for yesterday
For we do not know what
Tomorrow has in store
This scares us, for
It may be sheer delight
Or the most awful pain

We have the constant thought that
We may never make it there

So feel privileged for what you have today
And love everything in your life so deeply
For tomorrow it may be removed

"Life holds a true meaning for everyone
So travel the endless roads until you find it"

Troubled Times

Troubled times bring terrible tremors
My eyes tell of the suffering
They have held inside
They speak to you as if
There was only one story to tell

The story of me with all
My unpleasant
Physical sensations
That I hide from the world outside

I should let them be free
Soaring like an eagle
While instead I keep them
Under lock and key

I must release them
From my body's prison walls
Then the world will see
My crippled flaws
Like the glitch in my matrix

So now is the time to show the world
My true colours
For I have become

That soaring eagle

Embrace

Embrace me
Like no other has done before
Strip me back to bare raw bones

Slowly rebuild my torn heart
With stitches of love
Gently piece back together
My scarred, damaged body

Place your lips on mine
Bring back the colours
That had faded

Touch my face
So I know your affection for love
Then remember
To take a piece of my heart for you

Now open my eyes
So I can see who saved me
Then watch me
When I embrace you

My Journey

I open my eyes once more
All the sorrow has left my side

The scars stay from that journey just walked
A constant reminder of where I have been

So each will tell a different story
Of love
Of peace
Then pain
Then I will lock them away

My heart needs to heal
Because only I know
When the next chapter starts

Then my heart will be ready
To open up once more

"Time can pass us by in the blink of an eye
So value the little things this world has to give"

Flaws

See the sun breaking through me
Exposing all my cracks

Watch them glistening
Then dance with the sun

As they touch the ground
They bounce around

Making a broken man shine
For all to see the tears in the body he carries

Though he is proud of those jagged edges
He wonders when his maker will fix him
Or if he will be stitched by the next love found

For now he wishes to be whole
Once more
As he waits for the passing of the pain
That once was

Flames

Finally extinguished
Are the flames
That drive us wild

Smoke billows from my skin like The smoke signals of old

While none come to my rescue
Or see the distress call

So my core carries on smouldering
Burning every sense alive

From the shadows
Vultures appear
To take what they will
From this devastated body

Until there is nothing left
Of this exhausted life

Piercing Eyes

I see a future so bright
So free from dark

I see who I've become
By seeing your eyes pierce through me

A marvellous man stands before me
So intensely passionate but free

It has only been a short while since you touched me
Already I know my future lies beside you
Now time stands still while I breathe you in
A whisper I hear of who I am within

So gentle but nurturing
That must be me
Because you taught me to be free
Which breathed new life through me

Now I stand right before me I see
The amazing man is me
So this picture I see through your piercing eyes is me

"I could hold you till my last breath
But make sure you breathe into me before I'm gone"

This One

Shall this one carry you
When your legs become tired of life?

If so then this one should hold your hand
Through every approaching storm you encounter

This one will guide you to calmer waters
Where you can recover from life's stresses

And should this one say you will never be
Left feeling lost?
Because this one will be your guide
And compass

Should this one be the light in your life?

Through every dark cave you must pass
But this one will still be holding your hand

Then this one would love you more
Every day
And sit you on the highest throne in life
Which is beside this one

English Rose

Beautiful, She Is an English Rose

Flowered from within
But no compliment taken
Just the honest conviction
Of who she is

Constant smiles found within her aching soul
But rarely in her heart

Sombre eyes speak of years of pain inside
Yet just one look brought her back to life
Life returned to every corner of her dismantled soul

Then, floating on the wings of her new-found love The most
deliciously ethereal feeling
She carried in her heart

An English rose, she was dancing
In the new sun of her former life

Memories

My dear lady
Why leave so many memories
Scattered within me?

Every inch of my body
That you once touched
Remembers all

I miss the gentleness
I discovered in your delicate hands
The way you smiled
As you picked me up from the slumber
I found that was in me

It has not been long enough since then
To stop putting ink on to paper about you

When the time comes
I will remember fondly
Every last word I wrote

"The distance between us can never be measured
Because I carry you with me everywhere I travel"

Daughter

So much joyful delight
You've brought to our lives
A small bundle of pure happiness you are
You made us your parents
And you are our daughter

Never had we felt
So much unconditional love
For such a small bundle before
You became our daughter

The first time
We held you in our arms
We became complete
Our little family we now hold so dear
A life we now lead
Since you became our daughter

You have become the biggest part of us
For our love for you will always shine
And you will always be our daughter

Broken

Broken I am
That's me
No repairs are able
To bring me back from
Where I am
Lost right inside with no light
To guide my way

No hand to hold
To help me from this unilluminated place
So I will carry on digging deeper
Into my own self-loathing
Slowly ripping out every emotion
I once loved

Darker but darker still I get
Till I implode
Causing a greater mess
For broken I am
That's me

All My Love

All my love, which I give you
You will now hold as one love
Not a day will pass
When you should not hold my heart with yours
Nor will there be a time that I want to be apart from you

A love for you has grown
So warm in my heart
An embrace with you
Is all that I really desire

Nor do I ever want to become
Anything less in your eyes

This man who has been moulded by you
Never wants to lose you
For that man only exists for now

"The stability of the human race balances in the unforgiving universe
Expanding all the time for us to wonder what lies in wait
Moons come, unveiling new wonders"

Socially Awkward Boy

There I stand, alone in a corner of a vast corridor
While others travel so fast past me

No one notices yet this damaged soul I have
The demons that rule my conscious mind are better left
unseen
I look to myself
I have no friends

A socially awkward boy I see staring through me

I shut my eyes for a minute then take a deep breath in
These demons I must make my friends
But these demons might be me
So I begin a journey
Not sure what I will see

The vast world lies before me
Who will see me?
As I get older a few things change me

A socially awkward boy I see staring through me

I feel no fear or pain any more
My soul has left me

Standing in a corner once more a lifeless soul I see
No emotions I feel in my eyes
They are empty spheres of ice

The cold person I have become is not me
I shut my eyes once more and who do I see?

A socially awkward boy I see staring through me

Guardian Angel

You came to me in the dark unexpectedly
In images I had seen ahead of their time

I never expected you to be resting beside me
Like you are doing
Then from time to time
You catch me watching you sleep
Like that peaceful angel you are

For you are my guardian angel

Homeless

The cold starts to creep into fragile bones
He finds himself sitting against the same old shop doorway
While he gazes into an empty cup
That once was filled with life
His oldest friend stands on all fours by his side

Every passing stranger ignores his call for some warmth inside

This was once a man with a bright future
Slowly he was stripped of everything he once was
Right down to the shell of the man he's become

Now comes the time to survive one even colder night
Hoping that he will wake for another day in this ghastly world

So he remains in that old shop doorway
Dreaming of a life that once was

"These days become harder without your presence
In the mornings I wake early but the nights are long"

Strength

Worsening are these symptoms I carry
Just a ticking time bomb waiting to implode
It's time to stand tough against the tremors of the aftershock I
feel
Which is breaking down my brick wall

This winding road I now travel will turn so bleak
So this strength I must keep
Without courage I am merely nothing
So I shall place one foot in front of the other While walking this
painful road to recovery

Star

A star I see
But you are more

That's a woman hiding in a star
Where she holds sparks of stardust
Bringing light to where she's never been before

She is just a blank canvas
Waiting for her story to start

While she waits for me
To create an extraordinary masterpiece

For her life is now ready to be painted

Vow

A vow I shall uphold for the rest of my life

Take my hand
Run through open fields of happiness with me
Through the sparkling sun
That makes us dance with glittering rays

I see happier memories we will make
Through dancing in stormy puddles

Never forget to hold me with your warmth
On those cold winter nights

Then I shall be with you through every thunderstorm
That tries to rip right through you

The love we have been conquered by
Which grows at such a fast pace
Consumes my entire world

So I will keep this vow to her forever more

Wars

So many talks of peace but
Will war rage on?
A world in constant crisis
The threat of nuclear wars hang over the average man's head
However, the average man does not care for wars
For only peace he sees

The threat made by dictators we have all seen before
Which have made the masses revolt

As the human race stands separated
Not knowing what the future holds

Now the time is upon us to stand
For the freedom of every child this world loves

The children of the world we see
With pain held so clearly in their eyes

So we should all be looking at a future with peace in our hearts

"Sorrow only possesses the most minuscule part of my coming soul
But my coming soul holds enormous quantities of contentment
inside"

Uncomfortable

Pins with needles track through every limb
Making hands take the form of claws
No spasm goes unnoticed by naked eyes
As they look but stare uncomfortably

Watch a little more
It is OK

It's as if I am just sitting in a glass cage
For the world to judge my body
Which has many imperfections

No one will ever understand what happens inside

For I will show the world
Then make uncomfortable stares fun

Never Really Had Your Love

I never really had your love
Since you left it under lock and key
So it never came to any damage
As your heart you never let outside your castle walls
So it would never bleed or become fragile

For your defensive moat that kept everyone at bay
You were the ice queen of emotions

After the rare glimpses of what I saw at your core
I fell harder for you but could never conquer the walls
So the closer I came
The harder you shut down

Alive

Comes the time when we all need to travel on
It's always on our own because we need to heal
The lands might seem barren
Only they won't be barren for very long

Beauty will return to dazzle us once more
Then at that time we will welcome it back with open arms
As this is what we truly deserve
The light to shine upon our lives

Then breathe in every sweet aroma
The world has never let us forget
How alive we truly are

"You built your home on wild, free land
Like the gypsy girl you saw all those years ago
With scraggy hair and skin and bones so gaunt"

Venomous Tongue

Throw those insults
Make yourself feel better
I am not the only one to blame

You have also said harsh things
You call me selfish
You are the one out for yourself again

All you've done is judge everything that is talked about
Then you've continued to hurt me
With your venomous snake-like tongue

The only thing I remember you saying is You want to rid
yourself of this world
By taking all you have from your own life

I see with clarity that I am better off Without you in my life

Erased You

That's what I needed to do

Erased you from my life
Piece by piece so I may move forward
It has been hard
As I never wanted to let go

Now I see it's for the best
So I will close the book on this chapter
Then store it away

I will never utter your name again
As you have killed me time and time again

Now I will build my foundation once more
To start a new book in my life
This one will be without you

We Are Never Alone

Remember we are never alone
Someone is always guiding you
You might never see them

Be sure when you embrace the new-found glory
They have installed in you
Then run hard but fast as you can
With all your might

Never look back at the life that once was

Look to the distance
See the new light in your future
Spread your wings then soar high
Always believe in yourself
This will never make you fall

"So delicate is the heart that she possesses
But her soul must run wild and free"

Suicide

No more do I want to live
For no more do I want this pain
I just want to be empty from all within
Now I need to be at peace in my body

If that means the stars take me
Then I will shine with them but be free
Don't be sad or cross
For I can manage no more

I have battled for too many years
For I am so tired now
So let me lay my head down
Then close my eyes
I will rest in all your hearts

Till the day we meet again
I will be waiting for every last one of you
So I can hold you again
Therefore, for my last words I will say
I love you
Then goodnight

Broken Smiles

Broken smiles are all we see
People in pain smiling half-heartedly
Trying to be brave but just wanting to cry
Let the sorrow run down our faces

There is no shame in letting tears fall
That only shows the strength we have
Which proves we hide nothing from this world

So be strong
Never suppressing any emotion
Let it flow from every suffering we have
Ever endured without hesitation
Then we can release ourselves from the pain

Save Me

You saved me
Brought life back through smiles
Made me believe I could be
Whatever I wanted

You gave me
Courage to fight every day
You were always proud
Held my hand at every hurdle
To make sure I cleared away any troubles

Talked when moods got the better of me
But comforted when words had no help
Always showed me what I meant
By showing me your love
As nothing calms me more
Than when you're next to me

"Words striking the page are the lyrics of my soul
Defining who I really am"

Don't judge, as you won't understand

Yes, I stand alone in a fight no one sees
No one knows the enemies I shall battle with
Expect the warrior inside me

You will never walk in my shoes
So please don't try to understand the pain I carry

For sometimes the invisible war is only one person's battle

Here is just a small piece from my upcoming book.

On the Brink of Existence

Sometimes life can throw us unexpected curve balls. That takes us on a journey we never imagined travelling. But this journey might not have been our choice and there is nothing we can do to change it.

It might eventually break us or give us the strength and courage to overcome any obstacle.

That's exactly what happened to me.........

On the Brink of Existence

What life holds for us no one knows, except the vessel we are travelling in. We will become whatever we can, but some are destined to achieve certain things from birth. But, then again, life can throw us curveballs.

That's exactly what happened to me. The world was spinning on by, and I found myself sitting on a wall taking a breath in while drawing on my cigarette after another hospital appointment ...

But let me take you back to when this first started. I was nineteen, enjoying life and working hard but, yes, burning the candle at both ends. Don't get me wrong ... When life is going right, who doesn't?

When I was younger, I mean only by a couple of years, I never thought about which job I wanted. I found a passion for caring for people, so I jumped in with both feet.

That's when my life started spiralling out of control. One day I had an awful tremor that started to rise from deep inside me. I can only explain it as sitting on a plane at take-off. Every vibration was ricocheting off every muscle and bone in my entire body, just like your seat would shake in that plane at take-off.

Life returned to the normality I had come to know for several months, and I proceeded to work hard but continued burning life's candles at both ends. Little did I know that I was in for a roller coaster of storms. One night, when out with friends, my formerly strong hand picked up a drink but the glass slipped right through my hand, which I thought was clasping it, and smashed into a million pieces.

Everyone cheered at the sound of breaking glass. Embarrassed, I wheeled around on both feet and made my escape, as I felt the sound of breaking glass was my ego shattering in front of the eyes of a thousand strangers.

From then on I could slowly feel myself becoming clumsier. Tripping over my own feet was the worst thing. I never wanted to admit there might have been something wrong. But then never did I seek any attention from anyone close to me, as the socially awkward boy that I was has always been staring at me.

I threw myself more into my work until my world came caving in on me. It hit me hard. Well, that's what I've been told. Apparently it looked as though I was playing the Addams Family Generator arcade game. That makes you shake and thrash your head about, due to the electric shocks from the game machine.

It sounds like a right laugh, but that's when I left my vessel for three days. I'm not quite sure how, and maybe it was even longer in time. But, as time stood still, I could hear voices, but like a whisper from a girl trying to be sweet. Maybe it was the faint whisper of a breeze brushing my ear.

***

A loud voice approached from behind, shouting,

"Darkness descends over the forest."

Night had fallen. But at this time of year it should still be bright, with the sun flickering through the leaves, high in the sky like an eagle soaring.

Wyman, carrying the name of a fighter that also belonged to his forefathers (but he had yet to meet anyone in a fight), crouched down. He grabbed a handful of dirt, then threw it down to the ground like a wizard making a spell. This had been a long trek to try to find the tree of life.

Suddenly a crunching noise came from behind him. Cold metal pressed against his neck, and a gruff voice said,

"You have no need to travel in these parts."

Wyman hastily replied in his deep tone,

"We are simply looking for the tree of life."

As he stood up then turned he realised there was no one there. Bewildered, he continued to make his way steadily.

***

But then the onslaught of assessments came. The first was electroencephalography. It felt like something out of a sci-fi film, or even worse: Hannibal Lecter testing puppets.

Shortly after several episodes of the disease that left me hospitalised, they filled me with medication. I would rattle like a toy shaker you would give to a six-month-old baby to keep them occupied. When you did not you would get no peace.

But then, as if life was not going badly enough, I lost my freedom. How would you feel when pressing that pause button on life, freezing it right there? Because that day I lost my licence. I could not work any more after getting a diagnosis of epilepsy, but what would life hold for me from then on? I was unsure, as then my first bout of depression fired up.

This should have been the least of my worries. My tremors proceeded to inflict such destruction on my body that they would leave me battered and bruised from the inside out, like a fighter would feel at the end of a heavyweight fight. I can only imagine they would feel like that, but the scars my body now carries could tell a thousand stories. They are a constant reminder of what crippling pain this disease can inflict.

I found myself becoming more isolated from the world I had come to know, with fewer outings in daylight. A loner sat before me – not of my own making but of society's, by those who cast people aside as if we were stuck in times of old. But then again this could have all been caused by my first bout of depression.

I then found myself with a piece of cold metal pressed against my skin, and my next move would have been checkmated in a game of chess.

***

With the sound of heavy footsteps in front of me and Wyman shouting,

"We must push on to find the tree of life," the loud voice changed to a soft whisper.

"Stop getting down, riders."

In that instant four horsemen, all dressed in black, reared their horses up.

"We must find them. They are trying to draw from the tree of life its secrets, but we must stop them."

As the horsemen got further away, Wyman tapped me on the shoulder and spoke in his deepest tone.

"They are the guardian keepers of the tree of life, and how do they know we seek its secrets? Have you spoken to anyone about our trek?"

"No," I replied.

"Quickly, my brother, get to your feet. We must move fast and find some shelter from this darkness."

***

But I opted to just try and move the pain from inside my brain to somewhere not so damaging. This was the worst coping mechanism I could ever have thought of, as at this time things started getting choppy in the open waters of life.

I would find myself again with that same bit of cold metal pressed against my skin as if it had become my trusted friend to remove pain. I had no idea that this would be another part of my life spinning out of control, while at the same time I was looking down the barrel of the gun of life.

I woke one morning to cold creeping up from inside me, then running through my veins as if it were playing a game of chase with my entire body and crippling every movement deep inside. The strength I needed I could not find as one weary, depleted leg became my focus.

That's when I started losing my strength and turned into this struggling man who stands before me. The pain I saw staring back at me through the mirror was becoming me more and more.

On many mornings after this I came to understand that this could be far worse. Then anything to do with my new diagnosis of epilepsy but being too proud. I never wanted attention about any of the new things happening to me. Instead I would struggle like that first morning when I had felt like an ironing board, as I could not pull myself up to get out of bed. So I rolled over on to my knees instead, then crawled like I did all those years ago when I first started moving. Yeah, you could say I was embarrassed, but at that point I just had to prove to myself I could move. As the pain slowly drew itself back into the darkness of the caves where I dwelled I grabbed hold of myself. My subconscious then spoke and said,

"Pull yourself together, as I thought you knew you were stronger than this."

Just then my phone rang in the distance. It was from my love interest at the time but was not yet anything more. I did want it to be more, though. I never really did want to be alone at that dismal point in my life. But then maybe it really was not what I needed to think about just then as I should have just focused on myself.

I decided to do the opposite of what my brain was telling me to do, so I followed my heart into what I thought could be love. But oh, how wrong could I have been? It fizzled out so quickly, like a popped balloon squeaking through the air, until it was completely deflated.

But the hope dangled in my face that I would have a relationship, but removed it from my sight as I unravelled all my flaws. So once more I felt that constant stabbing pain right through my core that I had never come to understand from every previous time. I tried to love it. For maybe it was more companionship I sought, or maybe the thought of being able to talk to a friendly voice every other day when I found myself drawing more into myself.

***

"Come here, Wyman," shouted a girl from a small dwelling across the way. While my brother was looking at her he forgot that she was nothing but an ordinary girl. We have travelled far these last couple of dark days, but I thought she saw me and so I shouted back to her.

Wyman placed his broad arm around me and said,

"There will be many other conquests for you and the ladies of this world. We must stay here until the rain disappears, as the guardians will come to track us. And the fact that you move so slowly sometimes is a burden to you."

Wyman hesitated with a half-hearted nod, and I knew he was carrying the weight of this journey but refused to give up on my quest to find the tree of life, which might give me the answers that I had long hoped to be given. But maybe this tree had never really existed.

"My brother," he said, "get some sleep. You look weary and tired."

Printed in Great Britain
by Amazon

22053086R00076